YOUR BOOKS UNIQUE NAME:

# #

Search #NameOfTheBook to see where it has travelled to. Use Facebook and Instagram. Also use #TAOF when posting and searching to see the full world of *The Act of Friendship*.

First published in 2017
by JP O'Leary, Victoria, Australia

Author: O'Leary, JP, 1972.

The Act of Friendship
For young adults and up.
ISBN 978-0-9954348-2-0

1. Friends – journal, writing 1. Title.
Published by OLEARY72 Pty Ltd

Concept, Design & Layout: JP O'Leary

www.TheActOfFriendship.com

OLEARY72

The Act of Friendship
The gift of giving

by

JP O'Leary

Stop! Before you go any further name your book, if you haven't already.

Write the name of your book on the cover with a sharpie, starting with #TAOF so your new friends can photograph themselves with the book and post on Facebook or Instagram using the #NameOfTheBook.

When talking a picture of you with the book, go somewhere with a backdrop that highlights who or where you are, maybe it's your favourite park, restuarant or cafe. Perhaps it's the Eiffel Tower, Sydney Harbour Bridge or Kew Gardens. Just somewhere that is meaningful to you, it could be your office, school or backyard.

Where will your book travel to?

YOUR HEART AND MY HEART ARE VERY, VERY OLD FRIENDS.

THE ACT OF FRIENDSHIP

Do you remember pen friends?

The sound of the letterbox and the post falling onto the hallway mat in my parents home in Crawley, West Sussex, UK; memories from the 1990s, when as a teenager I would eagerly await a letter or small parcel from my pen friend Laura who lived in Los Angeles.

This was a time before email, mobile phones or digital cameras. I would take my photos carefully and when the whole roll had been exposed I would take it down to the pharmacy to be developed. I was usually impatient and so if I had the money I would pay an express fee and have my images developed within 24hrs. It seemed extravagant. But the overwhelming anticipation would otherwise kill me. How would my photos turn out? Would they be any good? Was i even in the frame? Had I over exposed them? Inevitably they would be badly framed and over exposed; back then we didn't we didn't have the ability to see what our photos were like in real-time, the ability to instantly delete and try again. We didn't have filters, Instagram, Snapchat or any of the myriad of apps we have today that improve our images at the click of a button.

These were candid and real. Looking back at them now, I still feel the magic of those moments captured in a split second of time, a time when you thought about what you photographed and those photographs became cherished memories, there were no do-overs. I laugh now at the way we posed. I laugh at the yellow roll necks and flares from an even earlier time, of photographs taken by my father. But each one was special, as each frame of film had an intrinsic cost and sanctity to it.

Flicking through the photographs as soon as you left the pharmacy was also part of the joy, the anticipation was too much, so standing in the rain under an umbrella I would hurriedly examine each photo. Choosing a suitable image to send to Laura, my pen friend in Los Angeles, was a big step. How would it represent me? Is this how I wanted to be represented? Back then you couldn't just take another selfie. These photos were planned and meticulously thought through.

Back at home I had an Amstrad 8512 computer; it had two 3.5" floppy disk drives, a green screen plus a dot matrix printer fed with a continuous roll of perforated paper that seemed never ending. I would never have dreamt of writing to my pen friend on the computer and printing out the letter on the dot matrix printer. My letters were written by hand, with care, love and much thought.

My handwriting though is terrible, so that made me think even more before putting pen to paper, it wasn't to be rushed. Often I would write down in my well worn notebook thoughts and ideas of what I wanted to say. In today's world it seems to be 140 characters or less or worse, just a selfie that is meant to speak for itself, shouting to the world the essence of your existence. It's about likes and social engagement, but that could just be a smiley face; a tacit exchange, meaningless and in itself empty, yet somehow many of us crave this social endorsement of our lives. We judge ourselves against other people's lives as lived out on Facebook and other social media channels.

I am equally guilty of all of this and judge no one for it. I just look to augment this with something more connected in a digitally focused world. I love seeing the images of friends and their families as they grow and expand over time from across the globe, but in many ways I am still out of touch with them, distanced by a keyboard, screen and digital bytes. The older we get the busier we get with competing priorities; whether family, work, or any combination of activities that draw us away.

Over the years I lost touch with Laura. I once had the opportunity to visit her in Los Angeles and we had a wonderful time, laughing and drinking red wine and she let me see her world through her eyes. Though time moves on and ultimately so do we. It reminds me that friendships can be fleeting, and although Laura and I are no longer in contact, she was a large part of my youth and one I do not regret for one millisecond, how can you regret ever being friends? I still miss the anticipation of receiving those letters and small parcels from Laura, the sound as they fell from the letterbox at my parents home. Her over exposed photos always made me smile.

Disconnect to connect

So what can we do? I am certainly not advocating completely removing ourselves from social media, though if that is something you want to do then I whole heartedly approve and wish you well. My addiction to Facebook is probably too strong at this point for me to extract myself from it fully. But we can disconnect in some simpler ways, and start a journey of new friendships and connection through stories. Stories that can traverse the globe and come back to you. Stories on paper that travel by post and unexpectedly fall onto your mat or appear in your mailbox.

That is *The Act of Friendship*. This little book of story prompts. It can ignite those feelings of the days of the sound of unexpected postal deliveries, the wonder of opening a package to discover its contents, your eyes wide open with hope and expectation.

'Paying it Forward' – the gift of giving

This is the benefit you receive from giving this book to others. You are giving wonder and joy to unsuspecting people and making new friends along the way. The hope and intent is that the book boomerangs its way back to you. That is the intent – boomeranging back to the originator, making you emotionally richer for the exchange. You may be a contributor, someone who this book has been sent to. If you are you have received this as an act of friendship, but you could be anywhere along the chain, you may be many degrees separated from the originator, and if all the story prompts except one have been completed then you are the last link in the chain and are asked to complete the last story prompt and send the book back to the originator, sending the book on its last journey, a journey home (their address should be in the back of this book) and clearly this has a cost to you in time and money, finding an envelope and then the cost of postage and taking to a post box or post office. I hope you can do this and I know the originator will be extremely grateful. This is 'Paying it Forward'. You receive the feeling of joy and accomplishment, as the book now completes its journey, full with worldly stories, it travels back to its originator for that last final surprise as they find it unexpectedly one day in the mailbox or on the mat.

As a contributor you may then decide to become an originator and start your own journey. A web of books that travel and make new connections is my ultimate goal.

No matter where you are in the chain I hope that you will take the time to take a selfie of you and the book showing the front cover and upload the image on Facebook & Instagram. Use both #NameOfTheBook (this should be on the front cover and the first page of this book) and #TAOF, this way, if for whatever reason the chain is broken and the book is lost in transit, there is a record of its journey. This is the digital version of the sound of the letterbox and post falling onto the mat with a thud that beckons your attention, the surprise and joy of randomness, finding out where the book is and with whom. This is one of the other reasons I don't advocate complete withdrawal from social media – we can create new 21st century feelings of surprise and anticipation as we check our virtual world daily to see where our stories have travelled to in the real world.

I encourage everyone to post and comment on these , take a moment to say thanks and engage with new people, explore the journey of the book, ask questions, find out what story they completed. Why did they choose that story prompt? There is also nothing wrong with posting your whole story, written out or photographed from the page. Enjoy and share.

Let's not lose the art of storytelling

Storytelling is fundamental to the human condition. They help us explore our thoughts and emotions, they help us to connect to one another. They help us grow and develop as people. Sharing cultures and ideas.

For most us we tell stories in our daily lives at work, from what we did at the weekend, to last nights TV or the latest news all told standing around the water cooler, still told orally from a long held tradition of verbal storytelling. We often don't take the time to write our stories down, to reflect and really consider our thoughts and emotions. The act of writing can be extremely therapeutic, it gives us the time to pause and reflect. These don't have to be the big ah-ah moments, those life changing moments, they can be small and intimate. They can be real or imagined or a hybrid weaving reality into fiction. We can let our imaginations run wild.

When we wrote to our pen friends, those were the moments that made us think and consider what was important, what stories we wanted to tell as we set out to put pen to paper. Because back then paper seemed precious and it wasn't so easy to edit. Now we type and hit delete multiple times again and again. I have done this many times while I write these introductory paragraphs for this book. We self edit. We often think too much or on the flipside too little.

But let's not prescribe how someone should enjoy and explore this book. If you can write by the seat of your pants, get your pen out, read the prompts, choose which one excites you the most and put pen to paper. You mostly have three pages to tell your story. Tell it your way.

Perhaps you are more methodical and want time to think and craft a story over time, or perhaps like me you just have bad handwriting, then I have created a word template that when printed, you can just cut out along the lines and glue into the book, it will fit perfectly. So you can take your time and hone your story. Download the word template here:

www.TheActOfFriendship.com/word

Either way is fine, it is about the act of writing, the act of friendship, your time and your consideration. Perhaps you are an artist and can tell your story through visuals, then do that, do what works for you. Write, draw, scribble or any combination. These are your stories and you can tell them any damn way you want!

So will you join me in this movement to bridge the virtual world with the real world? To tell stories? To make new connections? To embrace wonder, spontaniety, surprise and randomness? I hope so...

A LASTING GIFT

Our joint gift of giving

50c from every *The Act of Friendship* book will be donated to the Indigenous Literacy Found in Australia. This organization has a vision for equity of opportunity in remote communities across Australia, it aims to lift literacy levels and to instil a lifelong love of reading. 25% of Indigenous students in very remote parts of Australia are at the minimum reading standard this is compared to 90% of non-Indigenous students. To do this the kids need access to a range of different books.

There is nothing for you to do as an originator or contributor to *The Act of Friendship*, my hope has always been that your book will travel around the globe and so our Australian situation may be new to you, and you may have literacy issues from where you are from, so I encourage you to explore these and support reading and literacy programs where you are. If you would like to find out more about the Indigenous Literacy Found in Australia visit:

www.indigenousliteracyfoundation.org.au

Though if you purchased this book then you have indirectly made a donation, so find out how our little community has contributed, view our donation stats at:

www.TheActOfFriendship.com

We all have a story to tell. Start your story journey now.

JP O'Leary

INSTRUCTIONS

Option A

Keep this book just for you and use it as inspiration to fill it with stories.

Option B

1.) Give the book a name
2.) Write the name of the book on the cover
3.) Write your return address in the back of the book
4a.) Take a selfie of you holding the book, print, cut and paste it into the back of the book and share on Facebook using #NameOfTheBook
4b.) Take a selfie of you holding the book and share on Facebook using #NameOfThisBook and #TAOF write a post to go with it
5.) Buy a stamp and stick it into the TRAVEL HISTORY page and sign your name across the stamp or stick something else meaningful to you or your home country here
6.) Choose one of the pages and write, draw or scribble your story
7.) Choose a friend to send the book to and post it to them, you can add a note to explain how much their friendship matters to you

If you received this book in the post, you are a **contributor**, complete steps 4b to 7 above. Make sure to take the time to read the stories. The book for contributors is ephemeral, please keep it moving on its journey. The **originator** appreciates your support.

Why not start your own book? Or give a new copy as a gift for a friend to be the originator of their own journey of friendship:

Buy a new journey at www.TheActOfFriendship.com

TRAVEL HISTORY

NAME

AGE

MALE ◯   FEMALE ◯

TRUE ◯   FICTION ◯

CITY / COUNTRY

Never trust a man in a suede jacket

NAME

AGE

MALE ◯   FEMALE ◯

TRUE ◯   FICTION ◯

CITY / COUNTRY

Tears

NAME

AGE

MALE ◯   FEMALE ◯

TRUE ◯   FICTION ◯

CITY / COUNTRY

First day at school

FRIENDSHIPS BLOOM.

NAME

AGE

MALE ◯   FEMALE ◯

TRUE ◯   FICTION ◯

CITY / COUNTRY

It was in his best interests

She closed her eyes

NAME

AGE

MALE ○   FEMALE ○

TRUE ○   FICTION ○

CITY / COUNTRY

A picture paints a thousand words

(draw or write)

NAME

AGE

MALE ○   FEMALE ○
TRUE ○   FICTION ○

CITY / COUNTRY

He didn't move

NAME

AGE

MALE ○ FEMALE ○

TRUE ○ FICTION ○

CITY / COUNTRY

And then the door opened

NAME

AGE

MALE ○   FEMALE ○

TRUE ○   FICTION ○

CITY / COUNTRY

Lost in translation

NAME

AGE

MALE ○   FEMALE ○

TRUE ○   FICTION ○

CITY / COUNTRY

My Cat

(draw, write or stick a picture)

NAME

AGE

MALE ◯   FEMALE ◯

TRUE ◯   FICTION ◯

CITY / COUNTRY

Today at work
(draw or write)

GOOD FRIENDS ARE LIKE STARS.

YOU DON'T ALWAYS SEE THEM BUT YOU KNOW THEY ARE THERE.

NAME

AGE

MALE ⭘ FEMALE ⭘

TRUE ⭘ FICTION ⭘

CITY / COUNTRY

She held her breath, for what seemed like an eternity

NAME

AGE

MALE ◯   FEMALE ◯

TRUE ◯   FICTION ◯

CITY / COUNTRY

My last vacation

NAME

AGE

MALE ○   FEMALE ○

TRUE ○   FICTION ○

CITY / COUNTRY

Martha, Martha, Martha!

NAME

AGE

MALE ◯   FEMALE ◯

TRUE ◯   FICTION ◯

CITY / COUNTRY

My dog
(draw, write a poem or stick a picture)

NAME

AGE

MALE ◯ FEMALE ◯

TRUE ◯ FICTION ◯

CITY / COUNTRY

I placed the coffee cup on the table slowly and then looked up

NAME

AGE

MALE ◯   FEMALE ◯

TRUE ◯   FICTION ◯

CITY / COUNTRY

It wasn't me

NAME

AGE

MALE ○   FEMALE ○

TRUE ○   FICTION ○

CITY / COUNTRY

That feeling when you first
see your child

1 universe
9 planets
196 countries
1,000s of islands
7 seas

and I had
the privelege of
meeting you.

NAME

AGE

MALE ◯ FEMALE ◯

TRUE ◯ FICTION ◯

CITY / COUNTRY

There was a bump, then the
tyre went flat

NAME

AGE

MALE ○   FEMALE ○

TRUE ○   FICTION ○

CITY / COUNTRY

The look on his face

Life is better with unexpected friendships.

NAME

AGE

MALE ◯   FEMALE ◯

TRUE ◯   FICTION ◯

CITY / COUNTRY

My first kiss

NAME

AGE

MALE ○   FEMALE ○

TRUE ○   FICTION ○

CITY / COUNTRY

It started to softly snow.

When we stop looking, is when we usually find it.

NAME

AGE

MALE ◯   FEMALE ◯

TRUE ◯   FICTION ◯

CITY / COUNTRY

It was the night before Christmas

NAME

AGE

MALE ○   FEMALE ○

TRUE ○   FICTION ○

CITY / COUNTRY

Take a picture of yourself holding this book, print it out and stick it here

The last person to complete this book
please return it in the post to:

www.TheActOfFriendship.com

Do you have kids? Friends with kids?

The Act of Friendship KIDS EDITION

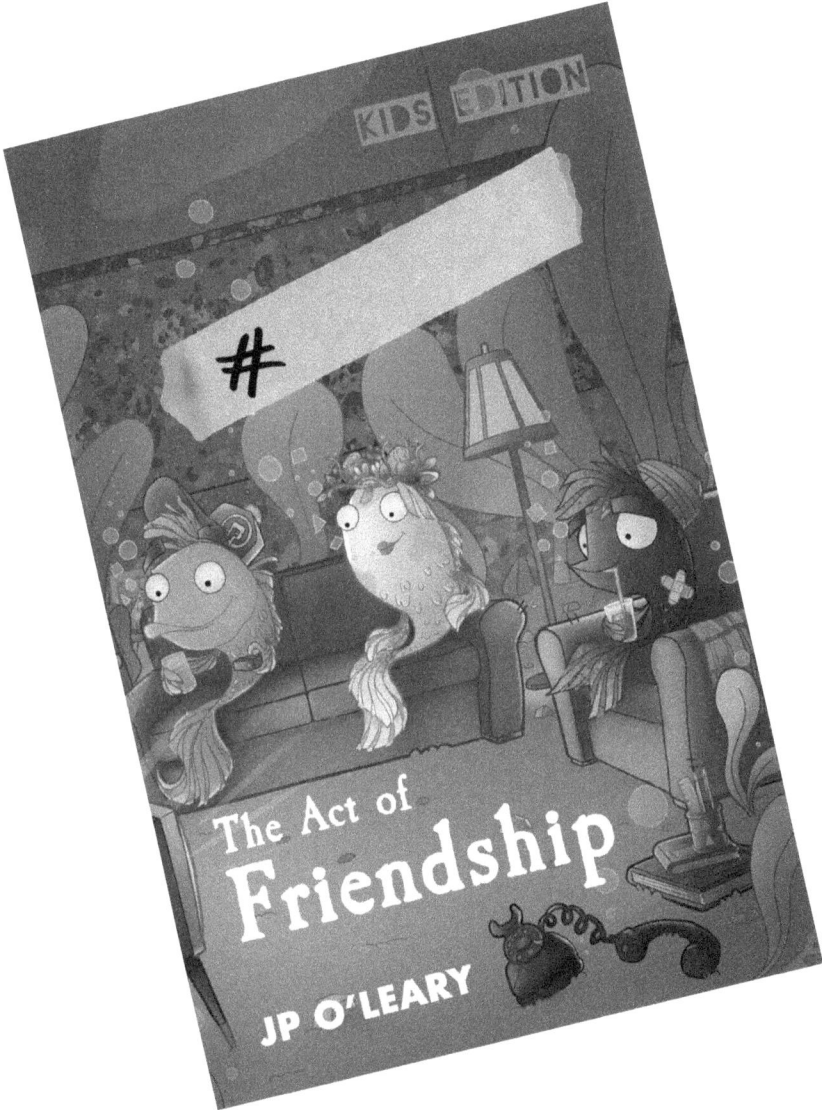

Register now for updates on the KIDS EDITION:

www.TheActOfFriendship.com/kids